12 GREAT TIPS ON
WRITING POETRY

by Yvonne Pearson

STORY
LIBRARY

www.12StoryLibrary.com

12-Story Library is an imprint of Peterson Publishing Company and Press Room Editions.

Produced for 12-Story Library by Red Line Editorial

Photographs ©: Florian Kleinschmidt/Picture-Alliance/DPA/AP Images, cover, 1; Nejron Photo/ Shutterstock Images, 4, 23; Maica/iStockphoto, 5; HamsterMan/Shutterstock Images, 6; Myimagine/ Shutterstock Images, 7, 28; d13/Shutterstock Images, 8; Chris Parypa Photography/Shutterstock Images, 9; mykeyruna/Shutterstock Images, 10; Javier Brosch/Shutterstock Images, 11; gbh007/ iStockphoto, 12; Loskutnikov/Shutterstock Images, 14; ra2studio/Shutterstock Images, 15, 29; mladn61/iStockphoto, 16; 360b/Shutterstock Images, 18; Eric Isselee/Shutterstock Images, 19; Lisa5201/iStockphoto, 20; pandasia/Shutterstock Images, 21; wichansumalee/iStockphoto, 22; TCreativeMedia/Shutterstock Images, 24; everest/Shutterstock Images, 25; Walter Albertin/Library of Congress, 26; Rido/Shutterstock Images, 27

Library of Congress Cataloging-in-Publication Data
Names: Pearson, Yvonne.
Title: 12 great tips on writing poetry / by Yvonne Pearson.
Other titles: Twelve great tips on writing poetry
Description: Mankato, MN : 12-Story Library, 2017. | Series: Great tips on
   writing | Includes bibliographical references and index.
Identifiers: LCCN 2016002320 (print) | LCCN 2016004498 (ebook) | ISBN
   9781632352750 (library bound : alk. paper) | ISBN 9781632353252 (pbk. :
   alk. paper) | ISBN 9781621434436 (hosted ebook)
Subjects: LCSH: Poetry--Authorship--Juvenile literature.
Classification: LCC PN1059.A9 P44 2016 (print) | LCC PN1059.A9 (ebook) | DDC
   808.1--dc23
LC record available at http://lccn.loc.gov/2016002320

Printed in the United States of America
Mankato, MN
May, 2016

Table of Contents

Read Lots of Poetry 4

Write about Things That Matter to You 6

Think about Why You're Writing 8

Choose a Cool Poetic Form 10

Paint Images with Sense Words 12

Transform Your Poetry with Metaphors and Similes 14

Make Poetry Sing with Rhythm and Rhyme 16

Pay Attention to the Sound of Words 18

Use Strong Verbs to Give Your Poem Zest 20

Revise: Write More than One Draft 22

Prime Your Imagination 24

Don't Be Afraid to Break Rules 26

Writer's Checklist 28

Glossary 30

For More Information 31

Index 32

About the Author 32

Read Lots of Poetry

It's easy to find poetry to read because it's all around us. Often, songs are poems—or poems are songs. Here's one you may know. It's a famous folksong written by Woody Guthrie:

> This land is your land,
> This land is my land
> From California
> To the New York island . . .

Playground chants also may be poems, such as "Ring around the Rosie, a pocket full of posies." And, of course, there are many books of poems. Poetry means different things to different people. It is a kind of writing that brings up strong feelings or shares ideas in interesting ways. Poems can also make people

Many musicians use poetic techniques to write lyrics.

Writers group poems together to create books, or collections.

think about something in a brand new way. The words in a poem are chosen carefully. They must say a lot in a little space, and they are often pleasant to hear.

One of the best ways to learn how to write poems is to read a lot of them. It is easier to write poetry if you are familiar with it. When you read lots of poems, your mind gets used to thinking about using words in new ways. You learn novel words and get ideas from others about expressing yourself in interesting, beautiful, and fun ways.

TRY IT OUT

Get a book of poems from the library. Ask the librarian to help you choose one. Or ask your teacher or your friends for recommendations. Read some of the poems and decide which one is your favorite.

Quick Tips

- Poetry is all around us.
- Poetry can make people think about things in new ways.
- Every word counts in a poem.
- Reading lots of poetry helps you learn how to write poetry.

Write about Things That Matter to You

Poetry allows you to express your thoughts and feelings. It also creates feelings in the reader. Of course, it's easier to create feelings in a reader if you care about your poem's subject. That's why it is important to write about things that matter to you.

Let's say you don't care at all about growing eggplants in a garden. If you try to write a poem about it, you will have a hard time thinking of anything to say. The poem will probably be boring.

Now let's say you love Halloween and love to dress up like a pirate. If you write a poem about being a pirate, you will probably be able to think of plenty of things to say. You will find

If you do not care about something, it will be hard to write about.

Quick Tips

- Poetry often expresses feelings.
- It's easier to express feelings in a poem if you care about your subject.
- Poems can contain any kind of feeling.

TRY IT OUT

Think about something you love— maybe a place, a toy, a pet, a food, a game, or a friend. Write four lines saying what you love about what you chose.

fun and funny words to describe your costume. You will be able to help your reader feel your excitement.

Poems do not have to be only about good feelings. Maybe you hate the taste of eggplant but have to eat some anyway. Maybe you are angry about it. Whether you love it or hate it, the eggplant matters to you, so you can write a poem that has those feelings in it.

Poems can be about any kind of feeling: happiness, sadness, anger, fear, or any other emotion. But many poets agree that poems should be about something that matters to the writer.

Poems can come from any emotion.

Think about Why You're Writing

People write poetry for many reasons. Sometimes people write poems to get their feelings out. They may feel sad or hurt or angry, and writing about it helps them heal. They may not want anyone else to read it. If you are writing for this reason, you don't have to think about whether anyone else will understand your writing.

However, there are other reasons for writing in which you will want to think about your audience. Maybe you want to write a poem to tell a friend how much you care about him or her. You will want to consider how your friend will feel when he or she reads the poem.

People tend to write differently for themselves than they do for others.

Poems sometimes commemorate big events, such as an inauguration.

Poems are also written to honor other people or to celebrate special events, such as weddings or graduations. At President Barack Obama's inauguration, Richard Blanco read a poem that he had written especially for the occasion. It must have been very important to him to express thoughts and feelings that were appropriate for the event.

Maybe you are writing a poem as an assignment and want to get a good grade. Then you will need to think about your teacher as the audience. Think about what you have learned about writing poetry as you work on the poem. If you want others to know what you're trying to say, it is important to think about whether your readers will understand the words and images with which you express yourself.

Quick Tips

- People write poems for many different reasons.
- Consider your audience when you write a poem.
- Choose words and ideas that your audience can relate to.

Choose a Cool Poetic Form

Poetry comes in many different forms. Different forms work in different ways. Most forms have rules that make them have a certain length, sound, or rhythm.

Haikus have three lines. Each line has a specific number of syllables. Syllables are the units of sound in a word. For instance, *kit-ten* has

two units, or two syllables. The first line of a haiku has five syllables, the second line has seven syllables, and the third line has five again.

Concrete poems are poems in which the words form a certain shape on the page. Often, the shape is what the poem is about. A poem about the moon might be shaped like a circle or a crescent.

Haiku is an ancient form of Japanese poetry.

Quick Tips

- Haiku, concrete, and acrostic poems have special rules to follow.
- Narrative, or prose, poems don't have many rules, but the words must still be chosen carefully.
- Trying out different forms leads you to new words and ideas.

MAKING A WORD A POEM

Here is an acrostic poem about a dog:

Digging in the dirt

On a hot day

Gives him a thrill.

An acrostic poem uses each letter of a word to begin a new line of poetry. For instance, if you write a poem about a dog, you could use three lines. The first line would begin with the letter *d*, the second line would begin with *o*, and the last line would begin with *g*.

Narrative, or prose, poems tell stories. Prose poems do not have many rules. But like all poetry, the words are chosen carefully to make the reader think about things in a new way.

Trying different poetry forms can lead you to new words and ideas. It might help you find exactly

the right word. For instance, say you are writing about gymnastics. The form you are writing in makes you find a word to rhyme with *tumble*. As you look, you discover *humble*. The new word gives you a new perspective on your subject. It opens up your imagination.

Acrostics are fun ways to describe people and animals.

11

Paint Images with Sense Words

We have five senses that we use to know what's happening in the world around us. These five senses are sight, taste, touch, sound, and smell. They let us experience the world. One of the best ways to recreate an experience in a poem is by using adjectives.

Let's say you take a walk in autumn. What are some of the things you know with your senses? You may see that the leaves are crimson red and lemon yellow. You may hear the sound of crackling as you step on dry leaves. You may feel the dry wrinkles of a fallen leaf when you touch

Being in nature can help people pay attention to their senses.

it. An earthy smell may greet your nostrils if you pick up a handful of damp leaves from the ground. When you get home, the sweet taste may delight you when you take a big bite of freshly baked pumpkin bread.

STRONG SENSES

What sense words stand out to you in the following poem, titled "Fall"?

My favorite thing about the fall

is when the sun

sets fire to the leaves,

making flames of red and gold.

It's the sweetness

that bursts in my mouth

when I crunch a crisp red apple

with my teeth.

No, I think my favorite thing in fall

is the feel of slippery seeds

pulled from the pumpkin's belly

before I carve a jack-o-lantern.

Or is it the scent of pumpkin pie

baking in the oven?

Oh my, fall is full of favorite things.

You can use adjectives to create images—pictures painted with words. Images make abstract words or ideas more real and understandable. For instance, *free* is an abstract word. A concrete image will make the idea of freedom come alive. "The kids felt free once their chores were done" becomes more alive with a concrete image. Look at the difference this concrete image makes: "The kids ran around and did somersaults when they finished their chores."

Quick Tips

- Human beings have five senses: sight, taste, touch, sound, and smell.
- We use our senses to understand the world around us.
- Sense words help readers experience what a poem is talking about.
- Poetic images are word pictures.
- Poetic images make ideas come alive.

13

6

Transform Your Poetry with Metaphors and Similes

Metaphors and similes are staples of poetry. They make readers see things in new ways. They also multiply the meanings in a poem.

Metaphors and similes are very much alike. A metaphor is a way of describing something by saying it is something else. "Winter is a scary beast" is a metaphor. A simile compares one thing to another by using the word *like* or *as*. "Winter is like a scary beast" is a simile. You probably don't usually think of a scary beast when you think of

Calling Earth a blue marble changes how we think of the planet.

14

winter. So you can see how the metaphor or simile makes you think of winter in a new way.

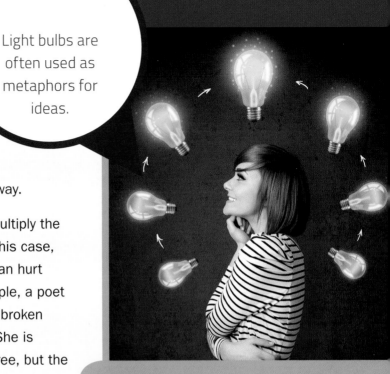

Light bulbs are often used as metaphors for ideas.

How does a metaphor multiply the meaning in a poem? In this case, it suggests that winter can hurt people. In another example, a poet says her family is a tree broken into pieces by a storm. She is talking about a broken tree, but the metaphor gives other meanings to the poem. She is also talking about her parents getting divorced, the family living in more than one place, and the pain of the experience.

Quick Tips

- Metaphors and similes make poetry fresh.
- They give poetry more layers of meaning.
- A metaphor is a way of describing something by saying it is something else.
- A simile makes a comparison between two things by using the word *like* or *as*.

THE BROKEN TREE

The storm was fierce.

It broke the tree

in three rough pieces,

laid them down

across the ground.

A broken trunk

with one lone branch

stood still.

But look!

That one lone branch

now wears

a new green necklace,

tender leaves to greet

a brand new spring.

15

Make Poetry Sing with Rhythm and Rhyme

Rhythm gives poetry its music. You can feel it when you read a poem, especially when you read it aloud. It's the poem's beat. You know you've got a strong rhythm when you find yourself wanting to clap your hands or tap your feet.

A poet creates rhythm with stressed and unstressed syllables. A stressed syllable is one on which you put more emphasis. For instance, *always* has two syllables (*al-ways*), and the first syllable is stressed. These syllable patterns are called feet. Many sentences in English follow similar patterns of rhythm. Listen for the rhythm in this line: "A cat will always chase a mouse." Do you hear it? Da-DUM, da-DUM, da-DUM, da-DUM. Some poems have a strict rhythm pattern, but some do not. You can choose what kind of rhythm you want to use when you write a poem.

Like music, poetry uses rhythm patterns.

FEEL THE BEAT

What rhythms and rhymes do you notice in this poem, called "At School Today"?

What rotten luck I had today.

My teacher took my ball away.

I only threw it at the door.

I did not mean to hit the four

small goldfish on her desk

that splashed

in all directions

when they crashed.

"Oh, what a mess!" she said to me.

"Go quickly. Get that bowl you see.

Pick up the goldfish instantly,

before they die. Go fast," said she.

Of course, I jumped

and bumped the shelf

that held her precious little elf.

Made of clay, it broke in half,

and all the kids began to laugh.

The teacher didn't laugh at all.

Instead, she pointed to the hall.

I'll miss my playground time—

oh, drat—

just because the fish went splat.

Quick Tips

- Rhythm and rhyme give poetry its music.
- You can create rhythm with stressed and unstressed syllables.
- You can use end rhymes, internal rhymes, and slant rhymes.

Rhyme also contributes to the musical feel of a poem. A rhyme is two words that have the same ending sound. *Jet* and *pet* rhyme. Sometimes, poetry has end rhymes. That's when the last words in two lines rhyme. Poetry may also have internal rhymes. This is when two words in the same line rhyme. "That fairy was very hairy" has an internal rhyme. Sometimes, poetry uses slant rhymes. A slant rhyme is an almost-rhyme, such as when two words have the same vowel sound or the same consonant sound. *Dear* and *door* are a slant rhyme. Some poetry doesn't use any rhymes at all.

17

Pay Attention to the Sound of Words

The sound of the words plays an important role in making poetry pleasant to hear. This does not include only rhyme and rhythm. Other techniques can help you create pleasant or interesting sounds. Playing with these techniques can be a lot of fun, and they can make your poem stand out.

Alliteration is when several words begin with the same first letter. Listen for the repeated beginning sounds in this sentence: "Stella saw a star last night and whispered a wish for new wings."

Assonance is when words use the same vowel sounds. Can you hear all of the short *a* sounds in these lines?

> A *crab* in the sea
>
> *stabbed* a *fat* little blob.
>
> Turned out he *grabbed* a
>
> water *rat*.

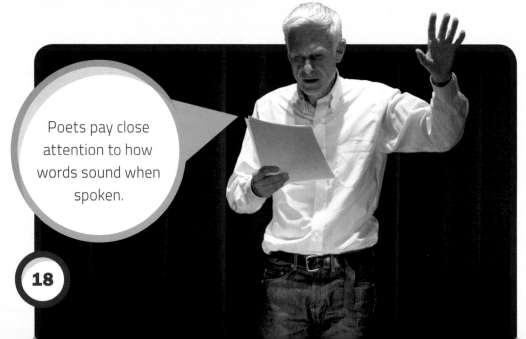

Poets pay close attention to how words sound when spoken.

These lines also show consonance at work. Consonance is the repetition of consonants in the middle or end of words. Can you find all the *b*'s in those lines?

Onomatopoeia is an especially fun technique to play with. It is found in words that imitate the sounds of the things they describe. Bees *buzz*, snakes *hiss*, leaves *rustle*, and water *gurgles.*

TRY IT OUT

Write a line using alliteration. Then, write lines that use assonance, consonance, and onomatopoeia.

Roar is an example of onomatopoeia.

Quick Tips

- The sounds of the words you choose make poetry pleasant to hear.
- Alliteration is when you repeat an initial letter.
- Assonance is when you repeat the same vowel in several words.
- Consonance is when you repeat the same consonants in the middle or end of words.
- Onomatopoeia is when words sound like what they represent.

19

Use Strong Verbs to Give Your Poem Zest

Strong verbs make strong poems. A strong verb is an interesting verb. It creates a more vivid picture for the reader. Here is an example: "The young girl walked slowly down the dirt path." We can replace *walked* with a stronger verb: "The young girl shuffled down the dirt path." *Shuffled* creates a more precise and interesting image. It takes away the need for the adverb *slowly*.

Which of these sentences uses the stronger verb?

The boy spoke loudly to his sister when she pulled his hair.

The boy barked at his sister when she pulled his hair.

You can also use the active form of verbs to turn them from weak to strong verbs. A verb can be active or passive. A passive verb tends to be a weak verb. This sentence uses a passive form of the verb *to pull:* "The giant wagon was pulled by a very small girl." The following sentence uses an active form of the same verb: "A very small girl pulled

Strong verbs create detailed images in readers' minds.

STRONG VERBS

Find the strong and active verbs in the following poem, titled "Oops":

Do you know what I discovered
digging through my locker
as I hunted for my homework,
clawed through papers—
math and spelling,
science, art, and history?
My fingers squished
through something soft,
something slippery.
I wondered, could it be?
That thing I needed
three weeks past,
when my stomach growled?
Oh, poor me! Once it was
a perfect apple that I plucked
fresh from our tree.
Now it's nothing but
a slimy mess, a rotten mitten
on my hand.

Quick Tips

- Strong verbs make more interesting sentences.
- *Shuffled* is a stronger verb than *walked.*
- Active verbs make poems more engaging and dynamic.
- *Is given* is a passive verb form. *Gives* is the active form of the same verb.

the giant wagon." Both sentences give similar information, but the sentence with the active verb is more dynamic. The focus is on the action and not the thing that was acted upon.

Active verbs don't bore the reader.

Revise: Write More than One Draft

It takes time to write a poem. You may think of an idea and tinker with it. Then you think some more and come back to it. You let the idea simmer in the back of your mind like a stew on a winter day. Sometimes it takes a few days or weeks. Other times it takes a few months. In fact, the poet C. K. Williams said it took him 25 years to write his poem called "The Hearth."

Returning to old ideas can spark creativity.

After poets have completed their first drafts, they usually come back again and revise their poems. First drafts are almost never perfect. In fact, don't be afraid to write bad poems. Bad poems can turn into good poems when you revise.

Put your poem away for a few days. Then, read it with fresh eyes. You will often notice things you didn't see before. Maybe an idea or a line is confusing. Or maybe a new and more interesting word will occur to you. Maybe the poem will seem too long and you will see a line you can get rid of.

Hearing from others is part of revision.

Give your poem to other people to read and ask them to tell you what the poem says to them. That will help you see if you are expressing what you intend to express.

Quick Tips

- Give yourself time to complete a poem. It may take days or even weeks.
- Most poets revise their poetry several times.
- Letting the first draft of your poem sit for a few days allows you to look at it with fresh eyes.
- Feedback from other people can help you revise and improve your poem.

Prime Your Imagination

People have different ways of getting themselves ready to write. A British poet, Edith Sitwell, used to lie in an open coffin to prepare herself for writing. Most poets don't take such strange approaches. But many have a ritual, like a special time of the day or a special place to sit.

You need quiet time to let the words and ideas of poetry bubble up to the surface of your mind. You need to daydream, but you need to pay attention to what's around you, too.

Poets also need to change their routines in order to get new ideas. If you can't think of anything to write, try writing in a new place. It can give you new ideas. Write in a library, a park, or even the kitchen. Doing different activities can also help. Go for a walk. Or draw a picture. Or listen to music.

Free writing is a technique that loosens your creativity. It lets you dig ideas out of

Poets spend time writing in places where they feel inspired.

Traveling can inspire creativity.

yourself that may surprise you. Take a notebook and a pencil and give yourself five minutes. Start writing about anything that comes to your mind, anything at all. Don't stop until the five minutes are up. The writing may not make a lot of sense. It may jump from one idea to another, or from one image to another. But it might help you think of things you have never imagined before.

Quick Tips

- Poets need quiet time to get a poem started.
- They also need to pay attention to the world around them.
- If you're stuck, prime your imagination by writing in a different place or doing something different.
- Free writing helps you think of new ideas and new ways of saying things.

Don't Be Afraid to Break Rules

One of the great things about poetry is that nobody gets too upset if you break rules. In fact, many famous writers break rules. Sometimes, breaking the rules can make your poems more interesting. One poet who is particularly famous for breaking rules is E. E. Cummings. He often used lowercase letters when punctuation rules required capital letters. In fact, because of this, his name is often written "e. e. cummings." He also made up words. In his poem about spring, "in Just-," he made up words like "mud-luscious" and "puddle-wonderful."

Still, it's important to know the rules and only break them for a purpose. Why do you think Cummings might have made up the word "puddle-wonderful"? We can't ask him, but we can guess. Perhaps it is a condensed way of communicating how fun it is to splash in springtime puddles.

Playing with words is one of the ways you can have fun when you're writing poetry. So is breaking the rules. You can try anything you can imagine.

E. E. Cummings

Breaking the rules of poetry can make your writing unique.

Write with long, run-on sentences. Disrupt the rhythm. Make up nonsense words. Write one-word lines. You could even try writing some words backward or upside down. And never forget to have fun when you're writing poetry.

TRY IT OUT

Make up five new words. Use some of them in a poem.

Quick Tips

- Many poets break rules.
- Breaking rules can make a poem more interesting.
- Before you break a rule, you should know the rule and only break it for a reason.

Writer's Checklist

✓ Read lots of poetry.

✓ Use poetry to express feelings, bad or good.

✓ Pick a subject you care about.

✓ Consider your audience.

✓ Try writing in different poetic forms.

✓ Use adjectives and create vivid images.

✓ Use metaphors and similes to give your poetry layers of meaning.

✓ Pay attention to how the words in your poem sound.

✓ Use rhythm and rhyme to make your poetry musical.

✓ Use strong, active verbs to make your poems more dynamic.

✓ Come back to your poem later and revise.

✓ Prime your imagination by changing your routine.

Glossary

abstract
An idea that exists in your mind but isn't a material thing.

adjective
A word that describes a noun or pronoun.

audience
A person or group of people who read or listen.

concrete
An actual or real thing.

condensed
To make something shorter or more compact.

crescent
A thin curved shape that narrows to two points.

dynamic
Something that is forceful or has energy.

inauguration
To introduce someone into a job by holding a ceremony.

novel
New and different from what you have seen before.

staple
An important part of something, almost always used.

For More Information

Books

James, Sara. *Writing: Stories, Poetry, Song & Rap*. Broomall, PA: Mason Crest, 2015.

Prelutsky, Jack. *Pigs, Pizza, and Poetry: How to Write a Poem*. New York: Greenwillow Books, 2008.

Sidman, Joyce and Rick Allen. *Dark Emperor and Other Poems of the Night*. New York: Houghton Mifflin Harcourt, 2010.

Visit 12StoryLibrary.com

Scan the code or use your school's login at **12StoryLibrary.com** for recent updates about this topic and a full digital version of this book. Enjoy free access to:

- Digital ebook
- Breaking news updates
- Live content feeds
- Videos, interactive maps, and graphics
- Additional web resources

Note to educators: Visit 12StoryLibrary.com/register to sign up for free premium website access. Enjoy live content plus a full digital version of every 12-Story Library book you own for every student at your school.

Index

abstract, 13
acrostic, 11
active verb, 20–21
adjective, 12–13
alliteration, 18
assonance, 18

concrete image, 13
concrete poem, 10
consonance, 19
consonant, 16–17,
    18–19
Cummings, E. E., 26

feet, 16

haiku, 10

line, 10, 11, 27

metaphor, 14–15
music, 16–17, 24

onomatopoeia, 19

passive verb, 20
prose poem, 11

revision, 22
rhyme, 11, 17, 18
rhythm, 10, 16, 18, 27

senses, 12–13
simile, 14–15
Sitwell, Edith, 24
slant rhyme, 17
stress, 16
syllable, 10, 16

vowel, 17, 18

Williams, C. K., 22

About the Author

Yvonne Pearson's poetry appears in many publications. She also writes essays and books. She lives in Minneapolis, Minnesota.